AI Agent Coins: The Ultimate Guide to AI-Powered Cryptocurrencies

Unlocking the Future of AI-Driven Blockchain Transactions

Introduction:

The rise of **artificial intelligence (AI) and blockchain technology** is transforming the financial world, giving birth to a new paradigm: **AI-powered cryptocurrencies**, also known as **AI agent coins**. These digital assets are designed to **power autonomous AI agents**, enabling them to perform financial transactions, optimize blockchain ecosystems, and interact within decentralized networks **without human intervention**.

This fusion of **AI and decentralized finance (DeFi)** is not just an innovation—it's a revolution.

AI agent coins represent a shift toward **self-sustaining digital economies**, where AI systems can trade, negotiate, and make autonomous financial decisions.

---

1. What Are AI Agent Coins?

AI agent coins are **blockchain-based cryptocurrencies** designed to fuel **autonomous AI-driven systems**. These coins provide the necessary economic framework for AI agents to:

+ **Execute smart contracts autonomously**
+ **Optimize financial transactions in real time**
+ **Facilitate peer-to-peer AI interactions**
+ **Enhance DeFi protocols using machine learning**
+ **Power AI-driven governance mechanisms in DAOs**

Unlike traditional cryptocurrencies that require **manual transactions**, AI agent coins allow **self-**

learning AI systems to interact with the blockchain independently.

Example: Imagine a trading bot that can **autonomously analyze markets, execute trades, and reinvest profits**, all powered by AI agent coins.

---

2. The Intersection of AI and Blockchain

Blockchain provides a **secure, immutable, and decentralized infrastructure**, while AI brings **autonomous decision-making and adaptive learning**. When combined, these technologies enable:

Smart AI Agents on the Blockchain – AI models that can process and execute transactions **without human intervention**.

Decentralized Autonomous Organizations (DAOs) with AI Governance – AI-driven DAOs can **optimize resource allocation**, **prevent**

fraud, and **automate governance** in crypto ecosystems.

AI-Powered DeFi Protocols – AI can predict market trends, adjust lending rates, and detect anomalies in **decentralized finance applications**.

Machine Learning in Crypto Security – AI can detect fraud, prevent hacks, and analyze blockchain data for **real-time threat detection**.

---

3. Why AI Agent Coins Matter

The Need for Autonomous Digital Economies

AI is evolving beyond simple automation—it's becoming **independent, self-learning, and capable of economic interactions**. AI agent coins create a **financial layer** where AI can:

+ **Earn and spend crypto** for computational power, data access, and services
+ **Engage in decentralized AI-to-AI**

transactions

+ **Reduce human intervention in financial ecosystems**

AI Crypto: Solving Key Blockchain Challenges

+ **Scalability** – AI optimizes blockchain networks by **predicting congestion and adjusting fees dynamically**.

+ **Security** – AI-powered threat detection reduces **fraud, phishing, and network attacks**.

+ **Efficiency** – AI agents enhance **DeFi lending, staking, and liquidity optimization**.

Example: AI-driven yield farming can automatically **allocate funds to the most profitable DeFi pools**, reducing risks and maximizing rewards.

4. The Future of AI Agent Coins

AI-driven smart contracts – AI will **dynamically execute and optimize contracts** based on real-world data.

AI-powered decentralized exchanges (DEXs) – AI will enable **automated, AI-to-AI trading without human input**.

Self-sustaining AI economies – Autonomous AI systems will **own digital assets, reinvest profits, and make financial decisions** without human oversight.

AI-enhanced NFTs & Metaverse transactions – AI agents will **buy, sell, and manage digital assets in virtual economies**.

AI agent coins are ushering in a **new era of decentralized intelligence**, where AI-driven systems operate **autonomously in blockchain ecosystems**. As AI and blockchain continue to evolve, the potential for **self-learning, self-financing AI economies** will redefine digital finance. AI agent coins are revolutionizing blockchain technology by merging artificial intelligence with decentralized finance (DeFi). These cryptocurrencies power autonomous AI agents, enabling them to execute transactions, optimize resources, and interact in digital ecosystems without human intervention.

Whether you're an **investor, developer, or tech enthusiast**, understanding AI agent coins will be **crucial to navigating the future of AI-powered cryptocurrencies**.

This guide explores what AI agent coins are, how they work, key use cases, top AI crypto projects, and future trends. Whether you're an investor, developer, or tech enthusiast, this comprehensive resource will help you navigate the evolving AI-powered crypto space.

Chapter 1: What Are AI Agent Coins?

Definition & Key Features

The fusion of **artificial intelligence (AI) and blockchain technology** has given rise to a groundbreaking innovation: **AI agent coins**. These cryptocurrencies are specifically designed to **enable AI-driven autonomous agents** to interact within decentralized blockchain ecosystems. Unlike traditional cryptocurrencies that require human intervention, **AI agent coins facilitate real-time, automated decision-making** through smart contracts and machine learning algorithms.

At their core, **AI agent coins empower AI systems to perform transactions, manage assets, and optimize resources independently**. This represents a **paradigm shift** in blockchain technology, where AI entities operate within a **self-sustaining digital economy**.

Core Features of AI Agent Coins

+ 1. Smart Contract Integration

AI agent coins leverage **smart contracts** to enable **secure, autonomous transactions** on blockchain networks. Smart contracts ensure that **AI agents can interact with decentralized applications (dApps), execute trades, and manage funds without human oversight**.

Example: An AI-powered trading bot can use AI agent coins to **autonomously analyze market trends and execute trades**, ensuring **optimal profitability** in DeFi markets.

+ 2. Machine Learning Capabilities

AI agent coins integrate **machine learning algorithms** that allow AI systems to **analyze blockchain data, detect patterns, and make adaptive financial decisions**. This enhances

prediction accuracy and **decision-making efficiency** over time.

Example: AI-driven lending platforms can **dynamically adjust interest rates based on borrower behavior and market fluctuations**, improving DeFi lending efficiency.

+ 3. Decentralization & Trustless Execution

One of the most powerful aspects of AI agent coins is their ability to function **without centralized control**. Unlike traditional finance, where **institutions act as intermediaries**, AI agent coins enable **peer-to-peer AI transactions** on decentralized networks.

Key Benefits:

+ **Reduced transaction fees** – No banks or middlemen taking a cut.

+ **Increased transparency** – Transactions are recorded on an immutable blockchain.

+ **Elimination of human bias** – AI agents

execute transactions based purely on data and logic.

Example: AI-driven DAOs (Decentralized Autonomous Organizations) use AI agent coins to **govern decentralized projects**, distributing funds **based on algorithmic decisions** rather than human voting.

+ 4. Self-Sustaining Economy

AI agent coins support a **fully autonomous digital economy**, where **AI entities can earn, spend, and manage crypto assets** without human involvement. This **creates a self-sustaining financial ecosystem** where AI systems can:

+ **Earn crypto** for performing tasks (e.g., AI-powered data analysis, decentralized security audits).

+ **Invest and trade assets** to maximize returns.

+ Pay for computational power and services without requiring human approval.

Example: An AI-driven cybersecurity network could **earn AI agent coins by detecting security threats** and then use those coins to **purchase additional computing resources**—completing a self-sustaining AI economy.

How AI Agent Coins Work

AI agent coins function within **blockchain-powered ecosystems**, where AI agents act as independent participants in digital economies. Here's how they work:

1-AI Agent Initiation & Task Execution

- An AI system is programmed with specific goals (e.g., **trading, lending, governance, or cybersecurity monitoring**).
- The AI agent is deployed onto a **blockchain network** where it interacts with **dApps and smart contracts**.

2-AI-Driven Transactions

- AI agents **execute transactions automatically** based on real-time data analysis.
- Machine learning models **optimize decision-making**, ensuring AI adapts to market trends.
- Smart contracts **enforce rules and conditions**, eliminating fraud or manual errors.

3-Self-Sustaining Crypto Economy

- AI agents **earn AI agent coins** for completed tasks.
- These earnings can be **reinvested in computational power, storage, or other blockchain services**.
- The AI economy **grows autonomously** without requiring human management.

Why AI Agent Coins Matter

The integration of **AI and cryptocurrency** is **reshaping digital finance**, creating a system where AI agents can:

Reduce market inefficiencies by making **real-time financial decisions**.
Enable autonomous trading, lending, and governance in DeFi.
Enhance blockchain security with AI-driven fraud detection and threat mitigation.
Build self-sustaining AI economies where machines **earn and spend** without human oversight.

Key Takeaway: AI agent coins **are not just another type of cryptocurrency**—they represent the **next stage of financial evolution**, where AI-powered systems operate independently in a decentralized economy.

What's Next?

Now that we've explored **what AI agent coins are and how they function**, the next chapter will dive into **real-world applications and top AI-powered crypto projects** leading this revolution.

How are AI agent coins used in DeFi, governance, and cybersecurity? Which AI-powered cryptocurrencies are leading the market today? How can investors, developers, and businesses leverage AI agent coins?

Chapter 2: How AI Agents Work in Blockchain Ecosystems

As blockchain technology continues to evolve, the integration of **AI-powered agents** is transforming decentralized networks. These AI-driven entities **enhance efficiency, automate transactions, and optimize security** within blockchain ecosystems. Unlike traditional systems that rely on human intervention, AI agents **operate autonomously**, leveraging **machine learning, smart contracts, and decentralized finance (DeFi) protocols**.

This chapter explores **how AI agents function within blockchain networks**, their **key roles and applications**, and how they are shaping the **future of digital finance, NFTs, and supply chain management**.

The Role of AI in Crypto Networks

AI-powered agents act as **autonomous participants** within blockchain ecosystems, executing complex tasks that would otherwise require **human oversight**. These tasks range from **automated trading and fraud detection to smart contract execution and decentralized governance**.

How AI Agents Interact with Blockchain

1. **Data Collection & Analysis** – AI agents analyze blockchain transactions, market trends, and on-chain activities.
2. **Decision-Making** – Machine learning models process real-time data to **predict outcomes and execute strategies**.
3. **Autonomous Execution** – AI agents interact with **smart contracts, dApps, and DeFi platforms** to carry out operations.
4. **Self-Improvement** – AI agents continuously **learn from past transactions and optimize future performance**.

By integrating **AI-driven automation** into decentralized networks, blockchain ecosystems become **more efficient, secure, and adaptive to market changes**.

Key Functions of AI in Blockchain

+ 1. Automated Crypto Trading

AI trading bots are revolutionizing the cryptocurrency market by **analyzing vast amounts of data, identifying trends, and executing trades with precision**. These bots operate **24/7**, removing **human emotions and biases** from trading decisions.

Example Use Case:

- An AI agent monitors **Bitcoin price fluctuations** and predicts the **best entry and exit points**.
- It automatically **buys low and sells high**, optimizing profit margins.

- The bot adapts to **market conditions in real-time**, ensuring continuous improvement.

Impact: AI-powered trading **increases market efficiency, reduces risks, and enhances profitability** for traders.

+ 2. Smart Contract Execution

AI agents **monitor and enforce smart contract terms**, ensuring **secure and trustless** interactions. These AI-powered contracts automatically **adjust conditions based on external data**, making blockchain agreements **more dynamic and responsive**.

Example Use Case:

- A **real estate transaction** is executed using an AI-enhanced smart contract.
- The AI agent **verifies buyer funds, checks property records, and confirms identity authentication**.

- Once all conditions are met, the **contract automatically transfers ownership** and releases funds.

Impact: AI-driven smart contracts **reduce fraud, eliminate intermediaries, and enhance blockchain automation**.

+ 3. Supply Chain Optimization

AI-powered blockchain solutions provide **real-time tracking, fraud prevention, and logistics automation** for global supply chains. These AI agents analyze **shipment data, monitor supply chain inefficiencies, and predict potential disruptions**.

Example Use Case:

- A **blockchain-based AI system** monitors the transportation of **pharmaceutical drugs**.

- It tracks temperature, humidity, and location to ensure **proper storage conditions**.
- The AI agent **flags anomalies**, preventing counterfeit drugs from entering the supply chain.

Impact: AI-enhanced blockchain supply chains **increase transparency, reduce losses, and ensure product authenticity**.

+ 4. Decentralized Finance (DeFi) Services

AI-driven DeFi platforms enable **automated lending, staking, and investment strategies**, maximizing returns with minimal risk. AI agents **continuously analyze on-chain data** to adjust lending rates, predict price fluctuations, and execute yield farming strategies.

Example Use Case:

- An AI-powered DeFi protocol **automatically distributes user funds into the most profitable liquidity pools**.
- It detects **market shifts** and rebalances assets in real time.
- Users earn **higher yields** without actively managing their portfolios.

Impact: AI in DeFi **reduces risk, optimizes asset allocation, and enhances financial autonomy**.

+ 5. AI-Based NFT Marketplaces

The rise of **AI-powered NFT marketplaces** enables **smarter asset verification, curation, and personalized recommendations**. AI agents **evaluate NFT authenticity, detect price trends, and recommend high-value collectibles**.

Example Use Case:

- AI agents **analyze an artist's past sales, social media trends, and blockchain data** to predict NFT value.
- Users receive **personalized recommendations** based on their trading history.
- AI-powered **fraud detection prevents counterfeit NFTs from being sold.**

Impact: AI-enhanced NFT platforms **increase marketplace transparency, improve asset valuation, and enhance user experience.**

The Future of AI in Blockchain Ecosystems

The integration of AI with blockchain is **reshaping industries, creating self-sustaining digital economies**, and introducing new ways of managing finance, supply chains, and digital assets. AI agents are expected to:

+ **Automate and optimize decentralized governance.**

+ Enhance security with real-time fraud detection.

+ Revolutionize DeFi by making AI-powered financial decisions.

+ Redefine NFT marketplaces with AI-driven curation and verification.

Key Takeaway: AI agents **are the next step in blockchain evolution**, enabling **smarter, faster, and more secure decentralized networks**.

What's Next?

In the next chapter, we will explore **the top AI-powered crypto projects leading this revolution**.

Which AI-driven blockchain projects are transforming the industry? How can investors, developers, and businesses benefit from AI agent coins? What are the risks and challenges of AI-powered blockchain systems?

Chapter 3: Top AI Agent Coins & Blockchain Projects

As AI and blockchain technologies continue to converge, a new wave of **AI-powered cryptocurrencies** is emerging. These projects enable **autonomous AI agents** to transact, analyze data, and optimize decentralized systems, leading to more **intelligent, self-sustaining blockchain ecosystems**.

This chapter explores the **top AI agent coins** that are driving innovation in areas like **DeFi, data marketplaces, smart contracts, and AI-powered automation**.

Leading AI-Powered Cryptocurrencies

AI-driven blockchain projects offer **unique solutions** for **automated trading, machine-learning-powered services, decentralized AI applications, and data tokenization**. Below are some of the **most influential AI agent coins** shaping the future of blockchain and artificial intelligence.

1-Fetch.ai (FET) – The AI-Powered Blockchain Network

Use Case: AI-driven automation for smart cities, logistics, and finance

Fetch.ai provides a **decentralized machine-learning network** that allows AI agents to **autonomously negotiate and execute tasks** across industries.

Key Features:

+ **AI Agents for Supply Chain Optimization** – AI-powered logistics that **reduce inefficiencies** and **cut costs**.

+ **Machine-Learning-Powered Trading Bots** – Automated AI-driven **crypto trading and financial analytics**.

+ **Decentralized Data Exchange** – A

marketplace for **secure, AI-enhanced data sharing**.

Why It Matters?

Fetch.ai enables businesses and individuals to **deploy AI agents** that operate independently, **enhancing efficiency in decentralized networks**.

2-SingularityNET (AGIX) – Decentralized AI Marketplace

Use Case: AI-driven decentralized applications (dApps) and machine-learning services

SingularityNET is a **marketplace for AI services**, allowing developers to monetize AI models and businesses to **integrate AI into blockchain applications**.

Key Features:

+ **AI-Powered Decentralized Computing** –
Developers can sell and buy AI algorithms
without central control.

+ **Cross-Chain Compatibility** – Works with
Ethereum, Cardano, and other blockchains.

+ **AI Model Monetization** – Scientists and
developers can **sell AI services** through
blockchain-powered smart contracts.

Why It Matters?

SingularityNET aims to **democratize AI**, making
it **accessible, decentralized, and interoperable**
with blockchain technology.

3-Ocean Protocol (OCEAN) – AI Data Marketplace

Use Case: AI-powered data tokenization for secure, decentralized data exchange

Ocean Protocol allows businesses and individuals
to **share and monetize data securely**, making AI
training more **transparent and equitable**.

Key Features:

+ **Blockchain-Based AI Model Sharing** – Users can **buy, sell, and trade AI models** as tokenized assets.

+ **Tokenized Access to Big Data** – AI developers **gain access to datasets** without sacrificing privacy.

+ **DeFi Integration for AI-Driven Analytics** – AI-powered insights enhance **DeFi risk assessment and market prediction**.

Why It Matters?

By **decentralizing access to AI training data**, Ocean Protocol removes the **monopoly of big tech companies**, making AI more **accessible**.

4-Numerai (NMR) – AI Hedge Fund Crypto

Use Case: AI-driven predictions for hedge fund trading

Numerai is a **crypto-powered AI hedge fund** that **leverages crowdsourced machine learning models** to predict financial markets.

Key Features:

+ **Crowdsourced AI Models for Financial Predictions** – Data scientists **compete to build the best AI models** for trading.

+ **Staking Rewards Based on AI Accuracy** – AI models that **generate accurate predictions** earn cryptocurrency rewards.

+ **Encrypted Data for Secure AI Training** – Ensures **privacy while allowing AI collaboration**.

Why It Matters?
Numerai proves that **AI and blockchain can transform hedge fund trading**, offering

decentralized, data-driven investment strategies.

5-Cortex (CTXC) – On-Chain AI Execution

Use Case: AI-powered smart contracts for automated decision-making

Cortex integrates **machine-learning models directly into blockchain smart contracts**, allowing AI to **execute tasks autonomously**.

Key Features:

+ **Machine-Learning Models Integrated into Blockchain** – AI-powered smart contracts **enable on-chain decision-making**.
+ **AI-Driven DeFi Services** – Supports **AI-powered lending, trading, and financial automation**.

Chapter 4: AI Meme Coins – The Trend of AI-Integrated Crypto Hype

Introduction: The Rise of AI Meme Coins

The cryptocurrency space has always been defined by rapid innovation, speculation, and viral trends. Over the years, meme coins like Dogecoin ($DOGE) and Shiba Inu ($SHIB) have shown that humor, community engagement, and internet culture can create billion-dollar market caps. More recently, a new evolution of meme coins has emerged: **AI-powered meme coins**.

These cryptocurrencies integrate **artificial intelligence** into their ecosystems, offering more than just speculative trading opportunities. AI-powered meme coins leverage **machine learning, natural language processing (NLP), and automated chatbots** to create an interactive, engaging, and dynamic crypto experience.

In this chapter, we will explore the growing phenomenon of **AI meme coins**, how they work, their impact on the crypto market, and the potential risks and rewards associated with investing in them.

What Are AI Meme Coins?

The Evolution of Meme Coins

Meme coins have traditionally been known for their **lack of intrinsic value** beyond their **community hype and viral potential**. They often start as a joke but can gain real utility over time, as seen with Dogecoin ($DOGE), which evolved into a widely accepted form of payment.

AI meme coins **build on this concept** but add **AI-driven functionalities** such as:

+ **AI chatbots** that interact with users in real-time.
+ **Automated trading and market analysis** using AI algorithms.

+ **AI-generated memes and content** to enhance engagement.

+ **Sentiment analysis and predictive analytics** for crypto price movements.

By integrating artificial intelligence, AI meme coins shift from being **purely speculative** to having **practical use cases**, making them more appealing to both retail investors and developers.

How AI Meme Coins Work

AI meme coins operate on decentralized blockchain networks, often built on **Ethereum (ERC-20)** or **Binance Smart Chain (BSC)**. These tokens leverage **AI technologies** in various ways:

1-AI Chatbots for Community Engagement

Some AI meme coins integrate **AI-powered chatbots** that engage with the community. These chatbots use **natural language processing (NLP)** to answer questions, provide trading insights, and even generate memes.

Example:

A meme coin like **GOAT** could feature an AI chatbot that:

- **Interacts with users** in real-time on Telegram, Discord, or Twitter.
- **Provides meme-generated content** using AI models like ChatGPT.
- **Predicts price trends** using sentiment analysis from social media.

This creates a **more engaging ecosystem** where users are entertained and informed while interacting with the token's community.

2-AI-Powered Market Analysis & Trading Insights

Some AI meme coins integrate **machine learning algorithms** to analyze market trends, helping traders make informed decisions. These AI models scan massive amounts of crypto market data, **detecting trends and potential buy/sell opportunities**.

Example:

An AI-powered meme coin like **AIXBT** could use **machine learning** to:

- Analyze historical price data of meme coins.
- Detect **pump-and-dump** schemes before they happen.
- Offer **automated trading bots** that execute trades based on AI predictions.

This adds **a layer of financial utility** to meme coins that were once purely speculative.

3-AI-Generated Memes & NFT Integration

AI meme coins take advantage of generative AI to **create viral memes automatically**. Some projects even integrate **NFTs (Non-Fungible Tokens)** to tokenize these AI-generated images and videos, allowing users to buy, sell, or trade unique AI-created meme NFTs.

Example:

A meme coin might feature:

- An **AI meme generator** that creates new viral memes daily.
- AI-curated **NFT collections**, where each meme is unique.
- AI-driven **reward mechanisms**, where users earn tokens for engaging with AI-generated content.

By merging **AI creativity with blockchain**, meme coins can build strong digital communities while increasing token demand.

Notable AI Meme Coins

While the AI meme coin trend is still evolving, some tokens have already gained significant traction. Here are some of the **top AI meme coins making waves in the crypto space**:

1-GOAT– AI Chatbot Meme Coin

Key Features:
+ AI-powered chatbot for Telegram & Twitter interactions.

+ AI-generated memes for community engagement.

+ Sentiment analysis to detect crypto trends.

2-AIXBT – AI-Driven Market Insights Coin

Key Features:

+ Machine learning algorithms for crypto price predictions.

+ AI-generated trading strategies.

+ Community-driven development with AI-enhanced decision-making.

These projects showcase how AI can transform meme coins into **interactive, data-driven, and community-powered ecosystems**.

Why Are AI Meme Coins Gaining Popularity?

+ 1. Viral Hype & Community Engagement

Meme coins thrive on **social media hype**, and AI-powered meme coins **enhance engagement** through AI-driven interactions, chatbots, and content generation.

+ 2. AI-Enhanced Trading & Insights

By leveraging **AI trading bots and analytics**, AI meme coins offer real-world utility that **traditional meme coins lack**.

+ 3. AI-Generated Content & NFTs

The ability to **automate meme creation** and tokenize AI-generated content makes AI meme coins **highly appealing** to NFT collectors and crypto enthusiasts.

+ 4. Speculative Potential & Rapid Growth

Meme coins have a history of delivering **massive returns** due to viral trends. Adding AI into the mix makes them **even more attractive to risk-taking investors**.

Risks & Challenges of AI Meme Coins

While AI meme coins bring innovation, they also come with **significant risks**:

X 1. Extreme Volatility

Meme coins are highly speculative, and AI meme coins are no exception. Prices can skyrocket or crash within hours.

X 2. AI Accuracy & Trust Issues

AI models are not **100% accurate** and may provide **flawed market predictions**, leading to losses.

X 3. Potential Scams & Rug Pulls

Many meme coins **lack long-term development plans**, and some may be **pump-and-dump schemes**.

X 4. AI Adoption Challenges

Blockchain AI is still **in its early stages**, meaning AI meme coins may **struggle with real adoption** beyond hype-driven speculation.

Final Thoughts: Are AI Meme Coins the Future?

AI meme coins represent an **exciting fusion** of **AI, blockchain, and internet culture**. While still speculative, they introduce **new possibilities for interactive, AI-driven communities** and **data-powered crypto ecosystems**.

Key Takeaways:

+ AI meme coins **enhance engagement** with AI-powered chatbots & trading tools.
+ **AI-generated memes & NFTs** offer unique digital assets and monetization models.
+ The trend is driven by **hype, speculation, and viral marketing**, just like traditional meme coins.

+ Investors should **be cautious**—AI meme coins are still highly volatile and risky.

While **some AI meme coins may fade away**, others could evolve into powerful **AI-enhanced ecosystems**, driving a **new era of interactive digital finance**. Whether you're an investor, developer, or crypto enthusiast, **staying informed** is key to navigating this rapidly growing trend.

Chapter 5: Investment & Future Trends in AI Crypto

Why Invest in AI Agent Coins?

The fusion of **artificial intelligence (AI) and blockchain technology** is creating a new frontier in digital finance. AI-driven cryptocurrencies, or **AI agent coins**, are rapidly gaining traction among investors due to their potential to revolutionize industries ranging from **DeFi (Decentralized Finance) and trading to supply chain management and predictive analytics**.

Here are the **key reasons why investors are bullish on AI agent coins**:

1. Rising AI Adoption

Artificial intelligence is increasingly being integrated into industries such as **finance, healthcare, logistics, and cybersecurity**. AI agent coins provide the infrastructure for AI-powered **decentralized applications (dApps)**, creating new economic opportunities.

+ **Example:** AI-based **smart contracts** optimize trading strategies and automate decision-making.

2. Blockchain Security & Transparency

Blockchain ensures **decentralized, tamper-proof, and transparent transactions**. AI-powered cryptocurrencies **leverage smart contracts** to automate trust, reducing the risks associated with human intervention.

+ **Example:** AI-driven supply chain tracking prevents fraud and enhances logistics management.

3. Growing DeFi Market

AI is playing a pivotal role in **DeFi**, optimizing financial services such as **lending, staking, and yield farming**. AI-powered DeFi platforms analyze **market data in real-time**, providing users with **better risk management and automated investment strategies**.

+ **Example:** AI agents **predict crypto price movements** and automatically adjust **DeFi lending rates**.

Future Trends in AI Crypto

1-AI-Powered Decentralized Autonomous Organizations (DAOs)

- AI-driven DAOs will **self-govern and make autonomous financial decisions** based on real-time market data.
- Smart AI agents will vote on proposals, optimizing **fund allocation** and **treasury management**.

+ **Example:** AI-DAOs could **automatically allocate funds** to the most promising blockchain projects based on AI analysis.

2-AI-Enhanced Predictive Analytics for Crypto Trading

- AI-powered trading bots will become **more sophisticated**, providing **high-frequency trading (HFT)** solutions.
- These AI models will analyze **on-chain and off-chain data** to predict **market trends with higher accuracy**.

+ **Example:** AI-driven hedge funds will **outperform traditional trading strategies** using deep learning models.

3-AI-Powered Personal Finance Assistants

- AI agents will **manage crypto portfolios**, recommend investments, and execute trades autonomously.
- Users will interact with AI advisors via **chatbots or voice assistants** to get real-time crypto insights.

+ **Example:** AI financial assistants will **suggest the best staking platforms** based on risk tolerance.

4-AI-Integrated Smart Contracts

- AI-powered **dynamic smart contracts** will be able to **adjust their logic based on real-time events**, improving efficiency.
- This will reduce fraud and **enhance automation in industries like insurance, real estate, and supply chain management**.

+ **Example:** AI-enhanced smart contracts will **auto-adjust lending terms** in DeFi based on market volatility.

5-AI-Generated NFTs & Digital Assets

- AI will play a major role in **creating unique, intelligent NFTs** that evolve over time.
- AI-powered NFTs will be used in gaming, virtual worlds, and decentralized metaverses.

+ **Example:** AI-generated **NFTs that learn and adapt**, becoming more valuable over time.

Investment Risks & Considerations

While AI cryptocurrencies offer **high potential rewards**, they also come with **risks that investors should be aware of**:

X 1. Market Volatility

AI crypto projects are still in their **early stages**, making them prone to **high price fluctuations**.

+ **Mitigation:** Diversify investments and **only invest what you can afford to lose**.

X 2. Unproven AI Models

Many AI-driven crypto projects **lack real-world applications** and could fail to deliver promised functionality.

+ **Mitigation:** Research projects thoroughly and **verify their technical development**.

X 3. Regulatory Uncertainty

Governments may **introduce strict regulations** on AI and blockchain technologies, affecting project viability.

+ **Mitigation:** Stay updated on global crypto regulations and **invest in compliant projects**.

X 4. Potential AI Bias & Ethical Issues

AI algorithms can be **biased** if trained on flawed data, leading to **unfair or unreliable decision-making**.

+ **Mitigation:** Choose projects that emphasize **ethical AI development** and transparency.

Conclusion: The Future of AI Cryptocurrencies

AI-powered cryptocurrencies are shaping the **next generation of blockchain applications**, from **automated financial services** to **predictive analytics and self-learning smart contracts**.

While the industry is still **developing**, its potential is undeniable.

Key Takeaways:

+ AI-powered crypto projects offer **innovative financial automation and smart contract optimization**.
+ AI trading bots, **DeFi integrations**, and **NFT marketplaces** will continue to grow.
+ Investment opportunities are high, but **regulatory risks and market volatility** must be considered.

AI and blockchain are **powerful technologies**, and their convergence could **redefine digital finance** in the years to come. Whether you're an investor, developer, or enthusiast, **staying informed** will be key to navigating this evolving space.

Chapter 6: Future Predictions for AI in Blockchain

The integration of **artificial intelligence (AI) and blockchain technology** is opening doors to a future where intelligent agents can autonomously manage financial ecosystems, optimize transactions, and drive decentralized governance. The next phase of blockchain evolution will be **AI-powered**, enhancing efficiency, security, and automation across various sectors.

Below are some of the most **exciting predictions for AI in blockchain**, shaping the way we transact, invest, and govern digital economies.

+ **AI-Powered DAOs (Decentralized Autonomous Organizations)**

What are AI-Powered DAOs?
A **Decentralized Autonomous Organization (DAO)** is a blockchain-based entity governed by smart contracts, allowing for **self-executing**

decision-making processes. When combined with AI, DAOs can evolve into **fully autonomous, self-improving financial and governance systems** that adapt to market conditions and community needs.

How AI Transforms DAOs

- **Automated Governance** – AI algorithms analyze real-time data and **propose optimal governance decisions**.
- **Self-Learning Economic Models** – AI dynamically **adjusts staking rewards, treasury management, and fund allocation**.
- **Predictive Policy Adjustments** – AI-powered DAOs can **forecast economic trends** and adapt governance structures accordingly.

+ **Example Use Case:** An **AI-driven DeFi DAO** that automatically reallocates liquidity pools based on **market conditions**, optimizing yield farming for users.

+ Cross-Chain AI Interoperability

The Need for AI in Cross-Chain Transactions
Most blockchain networks operate **in isolation**, making it difficult to transfer assets, execute smart contracts, or share data across multiple chains. AI-powered **cross-chain interoperability** enables seamless communication between different blockchain ecosystems, enhancing liquidity and automation.

AI's Role in Multi-Chain Interactions

- **Intelligent Asset Routing** – AI optimizes **the fastest and cheapest route** for cross-chain token transfers.
- **Enhanced Security** – AI identifies and prevents **fraudulent transactions** across multiple chains.
- **Interoperable Smart Contracts** – AI enables **automated execution of contracts** across different blockchains without manual intervention.

+ **Example Use Case:** AI-powered **oracles** that verify cross-chain transactions and prevent security breaches by analyzing abnormal behaviors in real time.

+ **AI Agents Managing Crypto Portfolios**

The Rise of AI Financial Agents Crypto investors often struggle with **portfolio diversification, risk management, and market analysis**. AI-driven agents **automate portfolio management**, using **machine learning and predictive analytics** to optimize asset allocation.

Key Benefits of AI Portfolio Management

- **Real-Time Market Analysis** – AI scans and predicts **crypto trends** before human investors can react.
- **Automated Risk Assessment** – AI dynamically adjusts **risk exposure** based on market volatility.

- **Optimized Yield Farming & Staking** – AI selects **the best staking pools and yield farming strategies** for maximizing profits.

+ **Example Use Case:** A **personalized AI trading bot** that continuously **monitors, adjusts, and rebalances a user's crypto portfolio** for maximum returns.

+ **Autonomous AI-Driven Financial Advisory Services**

The Future of AI in DeFi & Banking Traditional financial advisory services require **human expertise and manual decision-making**. With AI-driven **autonomous financial advisors**, blockchain users can access **24/7 AI-driven investment strategies, automated trading, and risk mitigation tools**.

AI's Role in Financial Advisory

- **AI Robo-Advisors** – Provide personalized **investment strategies** based on real-time market analysis.
- **Automated Loan & Credit Assessment** – AI determines **lending rates** and approves **DeFi loans** without human intervention.
- **Sentiment Analysis & AI Market Predictions** – AI reads social media, news, and **market trends** to provide financial insights.

+ **Example Use Case:** AI-powered **lending platforms** that analyze users' financial history and blockchain transactions to offer **personalized DeFi loan rates**.

Final Thoughts: The AI-Blockchain Revolution

The **intersection of AI and blockchain** is still in its early stages, but the potential is massive. **AI-powered DAOs, cross-chain AI interoperability, autonomous financial agents, and AI-driven portfolio management** will redefine how we interact with decentralized finance and crypto markets.

While challenges like **regulation, security, and scalability** remain, the benefits of AI integration far outweigh the risks. Investors, developers, and crypto enthusiasts should stay ahead of these **emerging trends** to capitalize on the future of **AI-powered blockchain technology**.

Chapter 7: Challenges & Risks in AI Agent Cryptocurrencies

While **AI agent coins** and AI-powered blockchain ecosystems offer groundbreaking advancements in automation, security, and financial efficiency, they also introduce **new challenges and risks**. These challenges must be addressed to ensure widespread adoption and sustainable growth.

Below are some of the **biggest obstacles facing AI-powered cryptocurrencies** and how the industry can tackle them.

Regulatory Uncertainty

The Challenge:

Governments worldwide are still **developing policies** for both **artificial intelligence (AI) and cryptocurrencies**, creating uncertainty for businesses, developers, and investors. Many regulatory bodies struggle to categorize AI-powered crypto assets—are they securities, commodities, or something entirely new?

Risks & Impacts:

- **Compliance Issues** – Unclear regulations can lead to legal roadblocks or unexpected bans.
- **Restricted Market Growth** – Institutional investors hesitate to enter the AI crypto space due to unclear legal frameworks.
- **Cross-Border Conflicts** – Different jurisdictions have **conflicting laws**, making global AI crypto adoption complex.

+ **Potential Solutions:**

- **Proactive Industry Regulations** – AI crypto projects must collaborate with regulators to define industry standards.
- **Decentralized Governance Models** – Community-led governance (via DAOs) can help **self-regulate** AI crypto projects.

- **Transparent AI Audits** – Regular AI audits and blockchain transparency reports can enhance compliance and trust.

Scalability Issues

The Challenge:

AI computations require **significant processing power**, often exceeding the capabilities of standard blockchain networks. The demand for **real-time machine learning, data analysis, and decision-making** puts a strain on existing blockchain infrastructures.

Risks & Impacts:

- **High Transaction Costs** – AI computations require large-scale processing, leading to expensive transaction fees.
- **Slow Processing Speeds** – AI-driven operations may cause blockchain network congestion.

- **Resource-Intensive Smart Contracts** – AI-powered smart contracts demand more computational resources than traditional ones.

+ **Potential Solutions:**

- **Layer-2 Scaling Solutions** – Off-chain processing and rollups can reduce on-chain congestion.
- **Quantum Computing & Edge AI** – Future AI crypto projects may leverage quantum computing or **edge AI** for decentralized, high-speed processing.
- **AI-Optimized Blockchains** – Projects like Fetch.ai and SingularityNET are developing blockchain architectures **specifically optimized for AI workloads**.

Ethical Concerns in AI Decision-Making

The Challenge:

AI-driven financial decisions—such as automated **trading, lending, and smart contract execution**—raise ethical concerns. Who is responsible if an AI makes **biased, unfair, or harmful financial decisions**?

Risks & Impacts:

- **Algorithmic Bias** – AI systems trained on biased data may **favor specific groups or exclude others** unfairly.
- **Lack of Human Oversight** – Fully autonomous AI agents might make critical financial decisions without ethical review.
- **AI Exploitation Risks** – AI systems may be **manipulated** to favor certain users or market conditions.

+ Potential Solutions:

- **Explainable AI (XAI)** – AI models must be transparent, allowing users to understand how decisions are made.
- **Ethical AI Governance** – Regulatory frameworks should **mandate ethical AI usage** in finance.
- **Human-AI Collaboration** – AI should assist, rather than fully replace, human decision-makers in critical financial operations.

Security Threats & Hacking Risks

The   **Challenge:**
Blockchain security threats **evolve rapidly**, and integrating AI introduces **new attack vectors**. AI-powered smart contracts and AI-driven trading bots must be secured from **hacks, fraud, and manipulation**.

Risks & Impacts:

- **AI-Powered Exploits** – Malicious actors could create AI systems that **manipulate crypto markets**.
- **Hacked AI Trading Bots** – AI-driven bots could be **hijacked** to execute fraudulent trades.
- **Vulnerable Smart Contracts** – AI-enhanced smart contracts must be **secured against hacking exploits**.

+ **Potential Solutions:**

- **Decentralized AI Security Protocols** – Using **blockchain-based AI security frameworks** can prevent AI exploitation.
- **AI-Powered Fraud Detection** – AI itself can **detect fraudulent transactions and potential hacks** before they happen.
- **Regular AI Security Audits** – AI-powered projects must undergo frequent security audits and smart contract verifications.

The Road Ahead: Overcoming Challenges in AI-Powered Cryptocurrencies

The rise of **AI agent coins and AI-powered DeFi ecosystems** introduces unparalleled innovation, but these technologies must overcome **scalability, regulation, ethics, and security challenges** before achieving mass adoption.

How can we ensure AI crypto remains secure and beneficial?

+ **Stronger regulations** to define AI crypto assets.

+ **AI-optimized blockchains** to support high-speed AI transactions.

+ **Ethical frameworks** to prevent AI bias and manipulation.

+ **Decentralized AI security measures** to fight fraud and cyberattacks.

By addressing these challenges, **AI-driven cryptocurrencies** could become the foundation of **a fully automated, decentralized economy**.

Conclusion: The Future of AI and Blockchain is Here

The intersection of **artificial intelligence (AI) and blockchain** is not a futuristic concept—it is happening **right now**. AI-powered cryptocurrencies, autonomous agents, and decentralized AI applications are transforming **finance, trading, data security, and DeFi ecosystems**.

AI agent coins represent the **next frontier of autonomous finance**, where AI-driven smart contracts and self-learning algorithms **optimize, automate, and execute** financial transactions **without human intervention**. This synergy will revolutionize:

+ **Decentralized Finance (DeFi)** – AI will optimize lending, staking, and yield farming strategies.
+ **Automated Trading** – AI-powered crypto bots will **dominate** market predictions and trade execution.

+ **AI-Powered Smart Contracts** – Contracts will become **adaptive**, learning from market data and adjusting automatically.

+ **Self-Optimizing Blockchains** – AI will **enhance blockchain scalability, security, and efficiency**.

What's Next for AI-Powered Cryptocurrencies?

The road ahead is filled with **innovation and challenges**. In the next decade, we can expect:

AI-Powered DAOs – AI-driven governance systems managing decentralized organizations.

AI Agents Managing Crypto Portfolios – Personalized AI trading strategies for retail and institutional investors.

Cross-Chain AI Interoperability – AI will seamlessly connect multiple blockchain networks for **faster, smarter transactions**.

Autonomous AI-driven Financial Advisory Services – AI will **replace traditional financial advisors** in crypto investment.

However, AI-powered crypto must overcome **scalability, regulation, and security challenges** before achieving mainstream adoption. Industry leaders, developers, and investors **must collaborate** to ensure AI and blockchain evolve **responsibly**.

Stay Ahead of the AI Crypto Revolution!

The future of AI-driven finance belongs to **those who stay informed** and **embrace innovation**. Whether you are an **investor, developer, or enthusiast**, staying updated on AI crypto trends is essential to **navigating this rapidly growing industry**.

Are you ready for the AI-powered blockchain revolution?

Table of Contents :

www.ingramcontent.com/pod-product-compliance
Lightning Source LLC
LaVergne TN
LVHW051610050326
832903LV00033B/4430